THE ULTIMATE CHRISTMAS SHOW (abridged)

Reed Martin
&
Austin Tichenor

BROADWAY PLAY PUBLISHING INC
224 E 62nd St, NY, NY 10065
www.broadwayplaypub.com
info@broadwayplaypub.com

"Critic's Choice! They tell me vaudeville died some time ago, but...the knockabout, anything for-a-laugh spirit of the ancient genre is alive and well. Agile and quick witted...there's no denying their ingenuity when it comes to grabbing comedy out of thin air."
Boston Globe

"Brought down the house with gales of laughter."
Theatre Mirror

"A pure delight from start to finish... Inspired madness!"
Broadway World

"Delightfully twisted holiday cheer. Christmas will never be the same once you share the holiday with the inspired lunacy of the masters of condensing the classics."
San Diego Theatre World

"Side-splitting!"
Nashua Telegraph

"THE ULTIMATE CHRISTMAS SHOW (abridged) will make your spirits bright, whether you joyfully embrace the upcoming season or get dragged into it kicking and screaming."
Broadway World

"Nothing less than hysterical!"
Zingology

"Side-splitting fun... A night of belly-aching laughter!"
New England Theatre Geek

"Gloriously irreverent style…a Christmas pageant gone horribly, hilariously awry."
Dallas Morning News

"THE ULTIMATE CHRISTMAS SHOW (abridged) [is a] zany, irreverent, side-sticker-inducing amalgam of vaudeville, improv and song. Thunderous, standing applause."
Arts Ala Mode—Charlotte NC

"The bad boys of abridgment are in fine comedic form…This rollicking romp lovingly skewers every holiday tradition you can imagine."
The Accidental Thespian—Washington DC

"These brilliant clowns take us on an irreverent but heartwarming trip through the holidays guaranteed to step on more than a few sacred cows and `misteltoes'."
San Diego Magazine

"Like no holiday show I have seen before…this trio of actors delivers a tour de force performance that left the room in stitches and exiting the theater still buzzing…an absolute delight!"
Edge San Diego

"Stunningly hilarious…a must see for your entire family!"
KDHX Radio—St Louis

"A complete delight!"
Two On The Aisle—HEC TV, St Louis

"It is a long time since I have seen an audience laugh as loud and as long as this. THE ULTIMATE CHRISTMAS SHOW (abridged) is a delight that will keep you smiling for days and a great way to get you in the true holiday spirit."
LGBT Weekly—San Diego

IMPORTANT NOTE

The use of the name REDUCED SHAKESPEARE COMPANY in any way whatsoever to publicize, promote, or advertise any performance of this script IS EXPRESSLY PROHIBITED.

Likewise, any use of the name REDUCED SHAKESPEARE COMPANY within the actual live performance of this script IS ALSO EXPRESSLY PROHIBITED.

The play must be billed as follows:

THE ULTIMATE CHRISTMAS SHOW (abridged)
by
Reed Martin & Austin Tichenor

For their contributions to the development of the script, the Authors wish to thank:

Matt Rippy; Jane Martin; Campbell and Cian Martin; Dee Ryan; Quincy and Daisy Tichenor; Alli Bostedt; Dominic Conti; Jennifer King, Jenn Rugyt, Dodds Delzell, Dan Saski, Chad Yarish, Phillip Ferrero, Rafael Manzo, Kyle Stoner, and the staff of Napa Valley Conservatory Theater; Charles Towers, Steven Leon, Emily McMullen, Tom Parrish, and the staff of Merrimack Repertory Theater; Neil Benson and Opus 3 Artists; Elaine Randolph; Sonoma Valley High School; Sebastopol Independent Charter School; Alan Harvey; Tony Ginesi.

THE ULTIMATE CHRISTMAS SHOW (abridged) was first workshopped and produced by Napa Valley Conservatory Theater (Jennifer King, Artistic Director), in Napa, CA from 23 September to 9 October 2011. The cast and creative contributors were:

Dodds Delzell
Dan Saski
Chad Yarish

Directors	Reed Martin & Austin Tichenor
Stage manager	Jenn Rugyt
Scenic design	Tim Holtslag
Costume design	Skipper Skeoch
Lighting design	April George
Sound design	Mark Osten, Matthew Cowell
Understudies	Phillip Ferrero, Rafael Manzo, Kyle Stoner

The official World Premiere of THE ULTIMATE CHRISTMAS SHOW (abridged) was produced and performed by the Reduced Shakespeare Company at Merrimack Repertory Theatre in Lowell, MA (Charles Towers, Artistic Director) from 25 November to 18 December 2011, where it set several box office records and became both the best-selling holiday show and the third all-time best-selling show in M R T's history. The show later ran from 5–23 December 2012 at San Diego Repertory Theatre, and has also toured across the USA every holiday season, including runs in Fort Worth, Anchorage, Charlotte, and St Louis. The cast and creative contributors were:

Reed Martin
Matt Rippy
Austin Tichenor

Directors ....Reed Martin & Austin Tichenor
Stage manager...Emily McMullen
Scenic design..Tim Holtslag
Costume design... Skipper Skeoch
Lighting design .... April George
Sound design....................... Mark Osten, Matthew Cowell
Props ....Alli Bostedt

San Diego Rep cast:

Michael Faulkner
Mick Orfe
Dustin Sullivan

FOR WHAT IT'S WORTH

This published edition uses the names of the actors from the original production, but we encourage you to use the first and last names of your actual actors. Similarly, you should use the names of actual towns, roads, highways, and airports near you when describing the winter storm closings.

We also encourage you to read the stage directions, which have been written by the playwrights to describe the business and physical moments used (successfully) in the original production. We also encourage you to *ignore* the stage directions if you want, but at least read them. They may give you clues about what's going on. And if your cast is more diverse than the original production, you may absolutely cut the references to "white guys".

There are several topical references in the script, the humor and relevance of which will fade over time. Permission is granted to update those references. This is not to say scenes should be rewritten (which is, in fact, strictly prohibited) but rather we're giving you permission to change a punch line or reference from "Lady Gaga" to...honestly, is anybody going to come along as fabulous as Lady Gaga? We think not.

In our experience, the script works best when it's performed simply, seriously, and passionately. That is to say, the script is funny so play it straight. But most of all, have fun and perform the show with energy and pace. It seems obvious but it bears repeating: the St. Everybody's Ensemble is driven by an urgent need to accomplish their herculean task in less than two hours. They're making it up as they go, pulling props and costumes out of whatever corner of the church they can. If your production's running longer than about an hour and forty-five minutes (including intermission), you're doing it wrong.

PROGRAM INSERT
[optional but highly recommended]

Saint Everybody's Non-Denominational Universalist Church
presents our annual
Multicultural Interfaith Holiday Variety Show and Christmas Pageant

Hosted by the
Saint Everybody's Ensemble

SCHEDULED TO PERFORM
(performers subject to change)

The Snowmen
Relaxed holiday hip-hop   Des Moines, IA

Confederate Christmas Carolers
Traditional tunes sung the old-fashioned way
                                             Charleston, SC

Saint Everybody's Holiday Newsletter & Church Bulletin   Saint Everybody's Church

Cleveland Castrato Choir
Singing their #1 holiday hit   Cleveland, OH

Yuba City Yuletide Society
Fun and festive frivolity from a pre-Christian time
                                             Yuba City, CA

Swingle Sisters Jingle Singers
As if the Andrews Sisters never died and only sang holiday songs   Little Rock, AR

Kwanzaa Concert Caravan
Celebrate the Seven Principles in Song & Story!
Oakland, CA

Muslim-American Ramadancers
Celebrating the Holy Koran through movement and dance
Dearborn, MI

Cirque du Sleigh
Christmas clowns & acrobats with a French-Canadian twist!
Montreal, Canada

Saint Everybody's Sunday Schoolers
Letters to Santa from our little ones
Saint Everybody's Church

Mary & Ed's Marionettes
Premiering a bold new work   Allentown, PA

Saint Everybody's Gift Exchange
A Saint Everybody's favorite!   Saint Everybody's Church

The Buffalo Bells
Ringing in the holiday season!   Buffalo, NY

The Billy Barty Ballet Company
Standing tall in the world of the dance   Sarasota, FL

FIFTEEN-MINUTE INTERMISSION

Saint Everybody's Ladies' Auxiliary
Holiday recipes and cooking show
Saint Everybody's Church

Saint Everybody's Ensemble
Performing their Christmas classic   Your City, Your State

The Christmas Boy Choir
Young voices raised in song   Boston, MA

Holiday Historical Society
From the North Pole Chamber of Commerce

North Pole, AK

Patrick Stewart's One-Man Christmas Carol
Starring the legendary Patrick Stewart   London, England

North Piddle & Happy Bottom Panto Players
An English tradition! Dorset & Worcestershire, England

Holy Strollers!
Holiday toddlers perform the Nativity story   Jackson, MS

ACT ONE

(Holiday decorations festoon the theatre. Carols play as pre-show music. A fully decorated Christmas tree sits down left. Its lights are hung but not on.)

(The backdrop consists of three panels that reflect three aspects of Christmas: A manger in Bethlehem with the star shining brightly above it; a hearth and mantle with a roaring fire, presents, and a wreath hanging above it; and a huge portrait of Santa Claus holding a bag of presents as flying reindeer are silhouetted against the full moon behind him.)

(Also included is a banner that announces "Saint Everybody's Annual Holiday Variety Show & Christmas Pageant!" in festive lettering.)

(AUSTIN, MATT and REED run onstage. Each stands roughly in front of the drop panel which represents his point of view.)

MATT: Hello!

AUSTIN: Thank you for coming!

REED: Good evening! Merry Christmas!

(The audience responds.)

AUSTIN: Happy holidays! Ladies and gentlemen, good evening and welcome to Saint Everybody's Non-Denominational Universalist Church, where all faiths are welcome because we'll believe anything. I'm Austin Tichenor.

REED: I'm Reed Martin.

MATT: I'm Matt Rippy and we are—

ALL: The Saint Everybody's Ensemble!

MATT: Once again, Saint Everybody's has asked us to put together and host the annual Multicultural Interfaith Holiday Variety Show and Christmas Pageant.

(They each hold copies of the program and refer to it.)

REED: If you'll all take a look at your programs, you'll see we've got a lot of great acts scheduled to perform tonight, from the Nativity Story performed by the holiday toddlers of the Holy Strollers, to my personal favorite, all the way from Dorset and Worcestershire, England, the North Piddle and Happy Bottom Panto Players.

MATT: We'll also be dazzled and delighted by the Christmas Clowns and Acrobats from Cirque du Sleigh, the Muslim-American Ramadancers, and the Billy Barty Ballet's annual holiday favorite, *Li'l Nutzy: The Elf Nutcracker*.

AUSTIN: And there'll be music! The Swingle Sisters Jingle Singers will be here tonight, as well as the Christmas Boy Choir from our Catholic friends over at Our Lady of Eternal Suspicion, and the Buffalo Bells will perform their big hit "My Christmas Ding-A-Ling".

REED: The three of us have also prepared a little performance for later this evening, but right now—

AUSTIN: *(Looking at his program)* Wait a second! Patrick Stewart is going to be here performing his one-man *Christmas Carol*?!

MATT: That's right. I booked him myself.

AUSTIN: Patrick Stewart? *The* Patrick Stewart?

MATT: Yeah, Patrick Stewart. The C P A from [*local joke town*].

REED: Anyway, they've asked us to make a few announcements.

MATT: First of all, please turn off all electronic devices: phones, hearing aids, pacemakers. Please locate the exit nearest your seat, it's probably the way you came in so it shouldn't be too hard. In the event of a fire, please exit the building *before* tweeting about it. (*To the section farthest from the doors*) You folks can probably just relax, it's a real fire-trap, you won't be getting out.

REED: Photography of any kind is not allowed during tonight's performance; it's not only illegal, it's just plain rude. And anyone caught texting, tweeting, or posting pictures to Facebook during tonight's performance will have candy canes forcibly inserted in places God never intended.

AUSTIN: We're so glad you could make it tonight. I know we're all worried about the severe winter weather we've been having, but we hope to have you out of here long before the next storm hits. So without any further ado—

MATT: Our first act tonight comes all the way from Des Moines, Iowa, bringing their special kind of relaxed holiday hip-hop.

REED: Ladies and gentlemen, please give a great big Saint Everybody's welcome to…

ALL: The Snowmen!

(*They exit. Nobody appears. They come out, confused, and introduce them again.*)

ALL: The Snowmen!

(*Nobody comes out.* AUSTIN *goes to the left wing.*)

REED: I'm sorry, ladies and gentlemen... *(To the booth)* Jenn, what's going on?

(AUSTIN confers with somebody just offstage, who hands him a piece of paper. The guys crowd around him.)

AUSTIN: *(Sotto voce)* There's a big storm. They've shut everything down.

REED: *(Sotto voce)* Both airports?

MATT: *(Sotto voce)* The [local] road and the [other local road]?

AUSTIN: *(Sotto voce)* Apparently.

REED: *(Taking the paper)* Ladies and gentlemen, apparently these winter storms have just gotten worse.

MATT: *(To the audience)* We've been in the back rehearsing all afternoon. We thought for sure today the weather would clear up.

REED: Gladys has just informed us that none of the acts scheduled to perform tonight have arrived yet.

AUSTIN: *(Into the wing)* Seriously? Nobody?

MATT: We should have seen this coming.

AUSTIN: That's right. I had a terrible time getting here but I thought...

MATT/REED: *(They heard this story)* Right, you did...

REED: *(Referring to the paper)* And another big storm is due to hit the area in about two hours.

MATT: Yeah, according to Fox News it's coming in from the right.

(AUSTIN and MATT confer then exit to opposite wings.)

REED: So...I guess, ladies and gentlemen, unfortunately this means we're going to have to cancel this year's show.

(The audience usually groans.)

AUSTIN: *(Calling from offstage)* Hold on, Reed! *(He wheels on a trunk from down left.)* They still might get here. And look, some of their trunks made it.

REED: Great! So?

AUSTIN: So until they get here, we can use their props. We put together the program. We know what tonight's pageant is *supposed* to be—

REED: We do?

AUSTIN: Yes we do. Ladies and gentlemen, we will not disappoint you.

REED: We won't?

AUSTIN: No we won't. Until they get here, we'll try our best to put on this variety show by ourselves.

REED: How are we going to do that?

(MATT wheels on a costume rack full of clothes.)

MATT: I found this rack of costumes back in the choir room.

REED: I still don't think we can do this.

AUSTIN: Reed, if we don't do this, we'll have to refund their money.

(Beat)

REED: Okay! Ladies and gentlemen, we will put on the best multicultural interfaith variety show that three Christian white guys can.

AUSTIN/MATT: Yes!

AUSTIN: That's the spirit. *(He rolls the trunk into the wings.)*

REED: *(Looking at* AUSTIN*)* I'm sorry. I mean two Christians and one Pagan.

(AUSTIN *shakes his head at the unfair characterization but decides to let it go. He and* MATT *confer, and grab baseball hats and sunglasses off the costume rack.*)

REED: All right, ladies and gentlemen, please bear with us, we'll be making this up as we go along, but in the improvisational spirit of Joseph and Mary finding a different place for our lord and savior to be born—

AUSTIN: Woah, Reed. I know it's Christmas but let's not get religious.

(REED *glares at* AUSTIN *and rolls the costume rack off.*)

AUSTIN: But yes, in that improvisational spirit—our first act tonight was supposed to be a performance by The Snowmen, so...

(AUSTIN *and* MATT *turn on the energy of the act they're trying to replace.*)

AUSTIN: You know, Matt, it's Christmas time, isn't it?

MATT: It sure is!

AUSTIN: And what's your favorite part of Christmas?

MATT: Christmas presents!

AUSTIN: And what's even better than Christmas presents?

MATT: Christmas *wrapping*!

AUSTIN: Kick it!

(AUSTIN *starts to beat-box. They put their caps on sideways and kick it old school.*)

MATT: *(Rapping)*
Well it's the story of Jesus, our Lord and savior
With a little bit of white boy hip-hop flava
There was Joseph, there was Mary
Summer turned to Autumn
And the Angel of the Lord came down upon 'em
Sayin'—

(They beat-box as REED *walks back in with an armload of costumes and puts a stop to this.)*

REED: Woah, woah, stop, stop! What are you doing?

AUSTIN: We're filling in. It's Christmas rapping. Get it?

MATT: This is what the Snowmen do.

REED: Why are they called The Snowmen?

AUSTIN: 'Cause they're white.

REED: Nobody wants to see white guys rapping, especially us.

AUSTIN/MATT: Come on…!

REED: No. Rapping is not an appropriate way to celebrate Christmas. Here, put these on…

*(*REED *hands out Victorian coats and hats, which they all put on. They look like characters from the Dickens Fair. Perhaps* MATT *wears a bonnet.)*

MATT: What's all this?

REED: The Confederate Christmas Carolers didn't make it, but their costumes and sheet music did.

MATT: The Confederate Christmas Carolers?

REED: Yes, the Confederate Christmas Carolers. Christmas should be celebrated with traditional Christmas carols.

*(*REED *hands them sheet music, perhaps in black music binders.)*

REED: Here, sing this.

MATT: But we haven't looked over the—

REED: It's traditional! Just smile and sing!

ALL: *(Singing)*
I'm dreaming of a white Christmas
Just like the ones I used to know
Where on all occasions

We see Caucasians
And no one who isn't white as snow

(MATT *and* REED *are shocked as they sing the inappropriate lyrics, but then start to calm down.*)

AUSTIN: *(Singing)*
White as snow

ALL: I'm dreaming of a white Christmas
With hope the same is true for you
May your friends be light colored hues
And remember that Christ was killed by—

(MATT *stops singing first, then* REED, *as they realize what the lyrics mean.* AUSTIN *remains oblivious to the end and finishes by himself.*)

AUSTIN: *(Singing)*
JEWS!
(Spoken) Merry Christmas!

MATT/REED: What?!

MATT: *(Aghast)* Who booked the *Confederate* Christmas Carolers?

REED: Do they spell it with three Ks?

AUSTIN: I booked 'em. Come on, that's a beautiful song.

MATT: Did you hear the words?

AUSTIN: I just like the music. I don't think about the lyrics.

REED: They're racist hateful crap.

AUSTIN: Wow, Judgy Judgerton. I'm open to *all* points of view. Hey—! *(Singing off another sheet)*
Rudolph, the Redneck Reindeer!
(Spoken) Everybody—

MATT/REED: Austin, stop it!

(REED *takes* AUSTIN's *sheet music and costume pieces.*)

REED: *(As he exits)* Do you even hear yourself?

MATT: Austin, this sheet music is made of actual sheet!

(MATT pulls out music in the shape of a hood with two eyeholes. The mask has musical notation on it. They both drop their music and remaining hip-hop gear and kick it offstage. REED re-enters with sheets of paper.)

REED: So Austin, you've never thought about the words to any Christmas carols?

AUSTIN: I just love how they make me feel. I don't care about their "meaning".

(REED hands the papers to AUSTIN.)

REED: Well, you should care. Here. Read these. Study these.

AUSTIN: Oh I will, thank you! Reed, I think you misunderstand me. I love everything about Christmas. It's the most wonderful time of the year. I love the trees, the lights, the carols, the mistletoe—

(MATT re-enters and crosses to the tree.)

MATT: The presents!

AUSTIN: The holly, the egg nog—

MATT: The presents!

AUSTIN: And all the characters! Santa Claus and Ebenezer Scrooge and the Ghost of Christmas—

MATT: Presents!

AUSTIN: And George Bailey and Frosty the Snowman and Rudolph the Red-Nosed Reindeer—

REED: And Jesus.

(Beat)

AUSTIN: Sure. Absolutely. Jesus, Yahweh, Mohammed, Harry Potter, the Flying Spaghetti Monster. I love 'em all.

REED: What? No! Christmas is about Jesus. "And there were shepherds, abiding in the field, keeping watch over their flock by night. And lo, the angel of the Lord came upon them, and said unto them, 'Behold, I bring you tidings of great joy. For unto you is born this day in the city of David a Saviour, which is Christ the Lord.'"

(During this, MATT notices the Christmas tree lights aren't on. He sees the end of the lights is unplugged from the extension cord. He connects them, but the lights still don't go on.)

AUSTIN: Amen. I love the Nativity Story. Let's get it on.

REED: Hey, be careful. The Nativity story is sacred.

AUSTIN: Yes, Reed: for Christians, Christmas is all about the birth of Jesus. But tonight's pageant celebrates *all* the winter holidays, from the religious to the secular. Because after all Christmas isn't just for Christians any more!

REED: Pagan.

AUSTIN: I'm not a Pagan. I'm a Utilitarian. I believe in God when it's useful. And I think we can all agree on what our favorite part of Christmas is?

MATT: Presents!

REED: Jesus!

AUSTIN: The annual family newsletter!

ALL: Yes!

(AUSTIN and MATT run offstage.)

REED: That's perfect, because I have here the Saint Everybody's Holiday Newsletter and Church Bulletin. In fact, let me just read the bulletin first... *(He pulls it out of his pocket.)* The Saint Everybody's eighth graders will perform Shakespeare's *Hamlet* in the Church basement Friday at 7 P M. Everyone is invited to attend this tragedy. Ladies, the Saint Everybody's rummage sale is a chance to get rid of things that are no longer useful. Please bring your husbands. And our annual pledge drive is underway. Our slogan this year is "I upped my pledge. Up yours." And now, this year's holiday newsletter comes to us from the Bolander Family.

(The light switches to MATT, *dressed in a suburban house coat and fancy coiffed holiday wig.)*

MATT/OLEANDER BOLANDER:

Dear everybody at Saint Everybody's:
It's been a big year for the Bolander family. Our son Evander Bolander is now the top student in his sixth grade class. Holding him back for four years has really paid off.

Our fifteen year old daughter Levander Bolander is dropping out of high school to go away to beauty college. Fortunately for us she's leaving behind her three beautiful children.

Husband and father Zander Bolander is looking forward to returning to the ministry once he finishes his prison term. His new church will need to be at least five hundred yards away from the elementary school. And what about me—wife and mother—Oleander Bolander? I continue to feel blessed every day for having such a beautiful family. May the holidays make you feel as happy as I do thanks to my new medication.

(Blackout. The lights rise as AUSTIN *enters wearing a stereotypically gay-looking outfit: tight T-shirt, exposed belly, neckerchief, spangly headband, and hot pink short-shorts with a mistletoe belt buckle.)*

AUSTIN: Ladies and gentlemen, Gladys just—

(AUSTIN *stops because the audience is laughing at his outfit. Not knowing why they're laughing, he glances around, then turns upstage. Across his butt is the word "Juicy". The laughs spin him back around downstage.*)

AUSTIN: *Anyway.* Gladys just told me that our next scheduled act has not arrived, so we won't be able to hear the Cleveland Castrato Choir singing "Christmas Without Bells". I'm sorry about that, but—

(REED *enters and sees* AUSTIN.)

REED: Uh, Austin. What are you wearing?

AUSTIN: Oh, do you like it? 'Tis the season!

REED: No, I mean—that's kind of a new look for you, isn't it?

AUSTIN: What, I'm just following the stage directions you gave me.

REED: What stage directions?

AUSTIN: *(Taking pages from back pocket)* Right here.

REED: *(Looking)* Those aren't stage directions.

AUSTIN: What are you talking about? *(Pointing to the pages)* It says right here, "Don we now our gay apparel". This is the gayest apparel I could find.

REED: That's not what that means.

AUSTIN: Are you sure? There's a lot of 'O come let us adore him' in this.

REED: "Gay apparel" means festive holiday attire, and the "Him" is the Baby Jesus we're supposed to adore. Those are not stage directions, they're lyrics from Christmas carols.

AUSTIN: Ohh! So I didn't need to go tell it on a mountain.

REED: No.

AUSTIN: I coulda stayed here.

REED: Yes.

AUSTIN: And the angels aren't stoned.

REED: What?

AUSTIN: The angels we have heard aren't high?

REED: No! They're *on* high! They're high above us!

AUSTIN: Then why are they in a sea full of egg shells? And who's Gloria?

REED: What?

AUSTIN: Look—Gloria, in egg shell seas, Day-o!
(Singing)
Christmas come and me wan' go ho-ome...
(Spoken) These angels are definitely tripping, brosef.

(MATT enters.)

REED: That's the phonetic spelling for *Gloria in excelsis deo*, which is Latin for 'Glory to god in the highest'.

AUSTIN: Ohh, it's *Latin*....

(MATT enters. REED notices AUSTIN's belt buckle.)

REED: Austin—is that mistletoe?

AUSTIN: Yeah.

MATT/REED: Eeww!

REED: A lot of Christmas lyrics mean something different than what you think they mean.

AUSTIN: Oh, that is such a relief. I did a Google search for 'round young virgin' and you do *not* want to know what I found.

(REED grabs the sheet music.)

REED: Give me that!

MATT: And then there's the creepiest Christmas carol of all time...

AUSTIN: What's that?

MATT: *(Singing)*
God rest ye merry gentlemen
Let nothing you dismay
(AUSTIN joins in singing.)

AUSTIN/MATT: Remember Christ our Savior
Was born on Christmas day
(REED joins in.)

ALL: To save us all from...
(Screaming like a heavy metal band)
...Satan's power!

(Thunder. Lightning)

AUSTIN: Wow.

MATT: That storm's getting closer.

(MATT exits. REED rips up the Christmas carol lyrics.)

REED: *(To the heavens)* Okay, point taken. There are just too many weird Christmas carols. There only needs to be one. *(He sings one phrase off of each scrap of paper. Note: The tune to this song can be found at https://www. broadwayplaypub.com/the-plays/the-ultimate-christmas- show-abridged/)*
Jingle bells, King Wencesalas
Fa-la-la-la-la, the first Noël
The ox and lamb kept time as good as they smelled
O Christmas tree of Bethlehem
O silent O holy night
The herald angels sing away in a manger bright...
Hallelujah!

(AUSTIN and MATT pop out of each doorway.)

MATT: And Hanukkah!

AUSTIN: And Kwanzaa!

ALL: Shave and a hair cut, two bits!

*(On "cut", R*EED *tosses the bits of paper so they fall to the ground like snow. They bow. A*USTIN *and* M*ATT exit.* R*EED takes out his program.)*

R*EED*: It's too bad the North Piddle and Happy Bottom Panto Players aren't here, because next to the Nativity Story, my favorite holiday tradition is the English Christmas Pantomime. Most of you probably aren't familiar with this tradition, but a panto is a performance of a popular fairy-tale interspersed with songs, audience participation, a villain...

*(A*USTIN *enters, scribbling on the pages of a short script. He has changed out of his gay apparel.)*

A*USTIN*: Reed, hang on. I'm putting the finishing touches on a traditional panto just for you.

R*EED*: I love pantos!

A*USTIN*: I know you do!

*(M*ATT *enters, holding some paper.)*

M*ATT*: I'll tell you what I love. The greatest gift of all.

R*EED*: Jesus?

M*ATT*: A Harley-Davidson Ultra Classic Electra Glide motorcycle.

A*USTIN*: What?

M*ATT*: Let's face it. Christmas is about presents. *(To the audience)* Am I right? Yeah! Free stuff is good stuff. It's my favorite holiday, second only to Thanksgetting! To make things easier for you guys this year, I went ahead and made out my Christmas list. *(He unfurls a long roll of paper with lots of numbers and figures on it.)* It's more of a spreadsheet, really. At the top is the Harley, but there's a large number of gifts in all price ranges to fit any budget.

A*USTIN*: A motorcycle?

MATT: It's only thirty-six thousand dollars.

AUSTIN/REED: What?!

REED: See, this is the kind of commercialism that's killing Christmas!

AUSTIN: Hang on, Reed, I know how he feels. When I was a kid I used to go to the mall and sit on the fat guy's lap and tell him my fantasies.

MATT: Santa?

AUSTIN: No, just some guy.

REED: Eww! Don't talk to me about Santa. He freaks me out.

MATT: Well, every year you guys give me crappy gifts that I end up throwing away...

AUSTIN/REED: What?

MATT: ...but if you look at my spreadsheet and compare the expense-to-joy ratio, with all the pleasure that Harley will give me, thirty-six thousand bucks is a bargain.

REED: See, this kind of commercialism makes me long for the old-fashioned Yuletide traditions.

(AUSTIN *runs off and returns with a box.*)

MATT: Oh, you want old-fashioned Yuletide traditions? Reed, you're in luck! A box of props arrived for the Yuba City Yuletide Society and I think they'll have everything you want— (*Digging through them*) Ah-ha! Here we are! (*Handing* REED *a stick of butter*) Happy Yule Tide!

REED: Why are you giving me this?

MATT: Are you kidding? Butter is one of the great gifts you could get in ancient pagan days. If you rub it on a door frame, the Norse Goddess of Fertility will eat it.

REED: What?

MATT: *(Handing* AUSTIN *bread)* Hold this loaf of bread and pour water over your head...

AUSTIN: Will do.

MATT: ...until I sprinkle your face with goat's blood.

AUSTIN: Got it.

MATT: Then we sing, dance, and feast on goat intestines!

AUSTIN: Mm, boy!

REED: What is all this?

AUSTIN: Reed, it's just what you wanted, it's a good old-fashioned Yuletide. Yuletide was a pre-Christian festival where we get many of our contemporary traditions, like mistletoe, gift-giving...

REED: *(Pulling out his program)* Knock it off! This is where the Swingle Sisters Jingle Singers were supposed to sing the *Twelve Days of Christmas.*

MATT: Now that's something they should totally ban.

AUSTIN: *(Getting rid of the Yuletide box)* Ban? Why?

MATT: I mean, I'm all about presents but who wants those crappy gifts.

AUSTIN: That's true. On Day One you get a Partridge in a Pear Tree. On Day Two, you get Two Turtle Doves. On Day—

MATT: Or wait—do you get Two Turtle Doves and a *second* Partridge in a Pear Tree?

REED: The lyrics are ambiguous.

MATT: Plus they're expensive! Again, going back to my spreadsheet... *(He takes it out)* According to the this year's P N C Christmas Price Index the cost of buying all the gifts in the song last year would have been twenty-three thousand, four hundred and thirty-nine dollars and eighteen cents *(Or recent updated figure. The P N C Christmas Price Index is a real thing. Google it.)*

REED: And a generous true love who repeats the gifts, like the song lyrics suggest, would buy three hundred sixty-four presents at a cost of over one hundred and fifty-five thousand dollars. *(Again, this figure goes up every year. Check out the P N C Index.)*

AUSTIN: Yeah, but Reed, I wouldn't call someone who gives all these gifts day after day a true love. I'd call him a stalker.

REED: True.

MATT: And besides, who even *wants* those stupid gifts? Nobody wants pipers piping. They want ponies and iPads.

AUSTIN: I want a new house with a swimming pool.

REED: I want two season tickets to the *(Best local sports team)*.

MATT: I want a Harley Davidson Ultra Classic Electra Glide motorcycle.

AUSTIN: Yeah, good luck with that. Uh, you know what?

(AUSTIN turns to audience members and gets specific answers. The guys help by asking questions for clarity.)

AUSTIN: Ma'am, what do you want for Christmas?

(She responds. They banter with her and repeat her answer.)

AUSTIN: And you, sir?

(He responds. Again they banter with the audience member and repeat his wish.)

AUSTIN: And young man, what do you want for Christmas?

(The boy responds. The actors respond as with previous audience members.)

AUSTIN: See, this proves my point. Nobody wants
Lords-a-leaping, maids-a-milking…well, some people
probably want…

REED: Wait. I've got an idea. *(Singing)*
On the first day of Christmas my true love gave to
me…
(He gestures to AUSTIN.*)*

AUSTIN: What are you—a house with a swim—oh!
(Getting it and singing)
A House with a Swimming Pool

REED: *(Singing)*
On the second day of Christmas my true love gave to
me
Two Season Tickets

AUSTIN: *(Singing)*
And a House With A Swimming Pool

REED: *(Singing)*
On the third day of Christmas my true love gave to me
*(*MATT's *on board now.)*

MATT: *(Singing)*
A big ol' honkin' Harley

REED: *(Singing)*
Two Season Tickets

AUSTIN: *(Singing)*
And a House With A Swimming Pool

ALL: *(Singing)*
On the fourth day of Christmas my true love gave to
me…

*(They point to the first audience member who sings his/
her suggestion again. If s/he mistakenly sings the fifth day
melody [which many do], they can correct him/her.)*

(They do the same thing with the second and third audience member, indicating that each should sing the item they previously mentioned.)

(As the guys complete the song, AUSTIN runs around the audience, putting additional people on the spot and getting them to choose—and sing—new gift ideas spontaneously. The guys repeat the list every time until they get through all twelve days. This is a tough memory exercise but if the actors forget the order the audience will always help them out.)

REED: *(To audience)* Everybody!

ALL: And a House with a Swimming Pool!

(When it's over, AUSTIN gets a paper handed to him from the wings.)

AUSTIN: What? Aw crap. Gladys says the storm's getting worse. They're probably going to close the roads in about an hour.

MATT: That means you folks might have to stay here tonight. Slumber party!

AUSTIN: *(Checking his program)* Okay! So the next act was supposed to be the Kwanzaa Concert Caravan, but they're not here yet, shoot…you know what? Wait a second— *(He exits.)*

MATT: If that storm really hits tonight, we'll have to save Christmas!

REED: Christmas'll be fine. It's just a storm.

MATT: Oh that's too bad.

REED: Why?

MATT: Because Christmas movies are awesome! All the best ones are about saving Christmas. Like *It's a Wonderful Life*—

REED: Yes, the moving story of the government shutting down a bankrupt savings and loan.

MATT: That's not the point. It's about the power of believing. Like *Miracle on 34th Street.*

REED: Yes, where I believe the post office enables a mentally ill old man to carry on his delusion that he's actually Santa Claus.

MATT: But you can't argue with the message of *A Christmas Carol.*

REED: That a big Christmas dinner can cure a terminally ill child? Or *Frosty the Snowman?* What kind of moronic snowman goes into a greenhouse? Or *Rudolph,* where the lesson is that it's okay to be different? What kind of socialist propaganda is that?

MATT: Is there any Christmas movie you actually like?

REED: *The Little Drummer Boy.*

MATT: That's never on anymore.

REED: That's why I like it.

MATT: What about *White Christmas,* where two song and dance men save a Vermont Inn owned by their former commanding general?

REED: Really—soldiers who like musical theatre?

MATT: Nobody asked and nobody told.

REED: Guess not.

(AUSTIN *enters holding a Kinara and a box of props.*)

AUSTIN: Found it! Happy Kwanzaa everybody!

REED: What is Kwanzaa?

AUSTIN: Kwanzaa celebrates African-American culture from December 26 to January 1. Each of these candles represents one of the Seven Principles of Kwanzaa—Unity, Self-Determination—

REED: I don't even know any black people who celebrate Kwanzaa.

AUSTIN: Reed, the term is "African-American".

REED: Sorry. I don't even know any black people who celebrate African-American. Look, Kwanzaa is very nice, but we're not black.

AUSTIN: So? We're not Jewish and we love show business.

REED: Austin!

AUSTIN: In fact, speaking of show business... *(He pulls a Menorah out of the box and holds it up.)* Happy Hanukkah, everybody!

MATT: Happy Hanukkah, and a rip roaring Ramadan! As the Muslim-American Ramadancers would have shown us, Ramadan celebrates the time when Muhammad received the Holy Koran!

AUSTIN: Yes, but nothing compares to Hanukkah—The Jewish Festival of Lights!

MATT: But Hanukkah's a minor Jewish holiday. It's only popular because it's close to Christmas.

AUSTIN: Hanukkah's better than Christmas. It lasts eight days!

MATT: But Ramadan lasts a whole month!

AUSTIN: But you have to fast from sunrise until sundown!

MATT: And you get to feast at night!

AUSTIN: Ramadan usually doesn't even happen in December.

MATT: So Jewish Holidays are better than Muslim Holidays?

AUSTIN: Well, clearly you think Muslims are superior to Jews!

MATT: You said we couldn't celebrate Ramadan!

AUSTIN: You tried to force us to celebrate Ramadan! Hannukkah teaches gratitude and compromise!

MATT: Ramadan teaches empathy and kindness!

AUSTIN: Arabs!

MATT: Jews!

BOTH: Ahh! *(They both exit to opposite sides of the stage.)*

REED: Ah, Christmas in the Holy Land.

(AUSTIN runs back in.)

AUSTIN: Is he gone?

REED: Yeah. That was great. Shalom.

AUSTIN: Asalaam Alaykum, my brother.

(They fist bump. AUSTIN strikes the box.)

REED: Yeah. A silent mausoleum to you too. *(Looking at his program)* Shoot. This was the part of the program where the acrobats from Cirque du Sleigh were supposed to contort themselves into the words "Merry Christmas" on a high wire.

(AUSTIN gets an idea; sotto:)

AUSTIN: Shoot. I'd like to see that. Hey, can I—?

REED: *(Sotto)* Sure. Yes, do that. *(He exits.)*

AUSTIN: Yeah, as I was trying to say, I had to fly in last night and almost didn't make it. Let me tell you what happened...

(AUSTIN tells his tale as the lights fade very slowly to a special.)

AUSTIN: Twas a night before Christmas, with such snow and rain
Not a creature was stirring, including my plane.
My carry-on was stowed in the overhead with care
In hopes this last-minute flight would still get me there

But with all of the lightning and thunder and showers
We sat on that runway for hours and hours
What should have been only a two-hour flight
Was becoming a journey that might take all night

It didn't start well. First, my shuttle was late
Then the airport was mobbed, which wasn't so great
And they gave me a middle seat, which was really a
drag
And charged forty-five dollars to check in my bag!

And then at security—so much emotion!
They unwrapped my presents! Made me throw out my
lotion!
And then when it looked like I'd just about make it—
The T S A groped me and laughed at me naked

I boarded last but that wasn't the worst
I walked past the snobs who were sitting in First
And sat through the safety shpiel, which is always a
bore—
Is there *anyone* who hasn't fastened a seat belt before?!

They charged for a blanket, charged for a pillow
Charged for a headset, and a seat in the exit row
And just when it looked like things couldn't get more
black
The jackass in front of me leaned all the way back

So: They ran out of food, they would not let us fly
They would not take us back, and would not tell us why
It really looked like we would never get going—
Oh, and *that's* when the toilets began overflowing

But out on the runway there arose such a clatter
I sprang from my seat to see what was the matter
Across my companion I reached like a flash
Said, "get outa my way," and threw up the sash

And what to my wondering eyes should appear
But a crazed flight attendant holding peanuts—and

beer!
He'd high-jacked the food truck so lively and quick
I knew in a moment he'd arrived in the nick

Of time. He pounded quite hard on the emergency
door
He forced his way in, and he got on the blower
He said, "People! You're the victims, you're not to
blame
But I'll tell you who is!" And he called them by name:

"On Delta! United! American, too!
On Southwest! Lufthansa! Aloha! JetBlue!
On Qantas! On Virgin! Alaska! Cathay!
SunCountry! ExpressJet! On British Airways!

On Frontier! On Spirit! On New Zealand Air!
To all of you airlines we hereby declare
Whether we fly frequently, or just now and then—
WE'RE NEVER FLYING WITH YOU EVER AGAIN!"

And before the sky marshal could tazer him down
He pulled the emergency slide and slid to the ground
As he did he knocked drinks and snacks off the shelf
And I cheered when he did it in spite of myself

We now could take off, with that nut off the plane
We soon would be home and never see him again
But I heard him exclaim as they dragged him away in
the night
"Merry Christmas to all, they just cancelled your
flight!"

(Fade to black. Light rises on MATT.*)*

MATT: The Saint Everybody's Sunday Schoolers were
going to read their Letters to Santa but they couldn't
make it tonight. Fortunately, we have tracked down a
number of letters to Santa written by people you may
have heard of.

(Light rises on REED.*)*

REED: Dear Santa: My brother always gets way more attention on his birthday than I do on mine. Can you even things out? I have been very good this year, but not as good as my brother who is always perfect. Sincerely, James, brother of Jesus.

(Light rises on AUSTIN.*)*

AUSTIN: *(Reading)* Dear Santa: Obesity is one of the leading health concerns in the US and we know you've got a little round belly that shakes like a bowl full of jelly. Would you be our new spokesman? Sincerely, Jenny Craig.

(Light rises on REED. *Note: His letter should be revised annually to reflect current events.)*

REED: *(Reading)* [2011] Dear Mr Claus: I would like to offer a formal apology on behalf of the State of Arizona for detaining you last Christmas for lacking proof of citizenship. In the future please obtain a work visa before entering the U S A. While I regret keeping you from your appointed rounds, you entered the U S illegally and took a job that should have rightfully gone to an American citizen. Sincerely, Jan Brewer, Governor of Arizona. [2012] Dear Mr Claus: While I appreciate you bring toys to all the children of America, I fear it's giving 47% of them a sense of entitlement. In the future, please only bring presents to children who don't really need them. Sincerely, Mitt Romney. [2015] Dear Mr Claus: Since you do not have a passport or a work visa, you are entering this country illegally and taking American jobs. When I'm President I will build a wall to keep you out. Sincerely—Donald Trump.

(Light rises on MATT.*)*

MATT: *(Reading)* Dear Santa: How ya' doin'? Can you bring me political relevance this year? I'll be keepin' an

eye on ya'! Remember, I can pretty much see the North
Pole from my house. Sincerely, Sarah Palin.

(Light rises on REED.*)*

REED: In 1897, eight-year-old Virginia O'Hanlon wrote
a letter to the editor of the *New York Sun* newspaper,
and—this is true—the Editor's response has since
become history's most reprinted editorial.

(Light rises on AUSTIN.*)*

AUSTIN: *(Reading)* Dear Editor: I am eight years old.
Some of my little friends say there is no Santa Claus.
Papa says, "If you see it in *The Sun* it's so". Please tell
me the truth; is there a Santa Claus?

*(*AUSTIN *and* REED *quietly exit as light rises on* MATT.*)*

MATT: *(Very sincerely)* Dear Virginia, your little friends
are wrong. They have been affected by the skepticism
of a skeptical age. They do not believe except what
they see. Yes, Virginia, there is a Santa Claus. He exists
as certainly as love and generosity and devotion exist.
Nobody sees Santa Claus, but the most real things in
the world are those that neither children nor men can
see. Nobody can conceive or imagine all the wonders
there are unseen and unseeable in the world. Santa
lives, and he lives forever. A thousand years from now,
Virginia, nay, ten times ten thousand years from now,
he will continue to make glad the heart of childhood.

(Fade to black. The lights rise on AUSTIN, *consulting the
program.)*

AUSTIN: The next act was supposed to be Mary and
Ed's Marionettes performing their bold new work,
Pinocchio's Christmas in Whales. Yeah… It's sort of a
mashup of Disney and Dylan Thomas…you know
what, they're not here and it's just as well, so let's skip
ahead to a Saint Everybody's favorite: the Christmas
gift exchange. Some of you may have participated in

one of these before. It's very simple. If you brought
a gift, you can just place it under the tree and take
another gift for yourself. We'll start.

(REED *has entered with two gifts.*)

REED: Here you go, Austin.

AUSTIN: Thank you, Reed. We'll place our gifts under
the tree and then take— You know what, we'll take
ours later so that you can have first choice.

(*They place their gifts under the tree.* MATT *enters.*)

MATT: Oh, presents! I *love* presents! Which one is mine?

AUSTIN: None of them. You have to give a gift to get a
gift.

MATT: What? That's a rip off.

REED: Those are the rules.

MATT: You're kidding, right?

AUSTIN: Nope.

(MATT *tries to take a present.*)

REED: Stop!

MATT: Seriously?

AUSTIN: Seriously.

MATT: I'm telling Santa.(*He sulks off stage.*)

AUSTIN: Actually, if you didn't bring a gift, we actually
have some gifts for sale out in the narthex, so you can
buy one, put it under the tree and take another present
for yourself. That way everybody can participate—

(*It's a fun idea to actually have inexpensive, wrapped
gifts for sale in the lobby. Your theater can also encourage
audiences to bring small, wrapped gifts to the show to use in
the gift exchange.*)

REED: So what now?

AUSTIN: Well, the first act was supposed to finish with the Buffalo Bell Choir and the Billy Barty Ballet Company, but none of them are here...

(MATT *has returned carrying a box, which he puts down center stage. It is full of objects that can make noise—a children's xylophone and stick, cow bell, duck call, siren whistle, pans and lids, party whistle, desk bell, slap stick, hand held sleigh bells, etc.*)

MATT: Okay! I got presents!

REED: Matt, where did you get that?

MATT: I bought it.

REED: Matt...

MATT: I found it by the back door.

REED: Is it the bells for the bell choir?

(AUSTIN *opens the box.*)

AUSTIN: Nope. It's just junk for the rummage sale.

(REED *sees something he likes and pulls it out. It makes noise, either on its own or by hitting it.*)

REED: Oh cool! (*He pulls something else out that makes noise—a children's xylophone, perhaps. He plays one note three times, then three more times, then one time, in the rhythm of* Jingle Bells.) Name that tune.

MATT: *In A Gadda Da Vida?*

REED: Close. Listen again.

(*As* REED *does the same rhythm again,* AUSTIN *walks back to center and pulls out a different object and hits it, adding the right note at the end of the phrase. It's clearly* Jingle Bells.)

MATT: *Jingle Bells?*

REED: Yes. Here. (*Tossing him a toy from the box*) Go play.

(MATT *exits.*)

AUSTIN: You know what, pull the rest of that stuff out…

(*As* AUSTIN *runs off and returns with the rolling trunks,* REED *pulls more junk out of the box and arranges it on the trunks, banging each piece to see what noise it makes.*)

REED: Why? What are you doing?

AUSTIN: Here, spread these out. Okay, start again. Go slow.

(REED *plays the notes he played earlier.* AUSTIN *joins in using the notes created by the various other objects. They get as far as the first "…jingle all the way." You'll have to experiment to find different noise-making objects that play the actual notes of* Jingle Bells.)

AUSTIN: (*Proudly*) Huh?

REED: Nice! Let's see if we can keep going.

(*They play the second phrase of the song, ending with "…in a one-horse open sleigh" as* MATT *wanders back on. In the rhythm of the song he says:*)

MATT: (*Impressed*) Hey!

(MATT *crowds* AUSTIN, *turning the ratchet and ringing a desk bell, or banging on something else.*)

AUSTIN: (*Pushing him away*) Get away!

REED: Okay, let's start again from the top and this time, really burn.

(*Slowly and carefully,* AUSTIN *and* REED *play the song all the way through with* MATT *adding the occasional funny sound. They finish.*)

ALL: Hey!

(*As the audience applauds,* MATT *pulls a guitar or ukulele out of the box, or finds it backstage and brings it on.*)

MATT: Cool!

AUSTIN: Who's throwing that out?

MATT: I don't know but it's mine now.

REED: Does it play *Jingle Bells*?

MATT: Let's see… *(He plays the familiar rhythm.)* It sure does!

(MATT plays Jingle Bells, *with* AUSTIN *singing and* REED *accompanying with his various noise-making devices.)*

AUSTIN: Dashing through the snow
In a one horse open sleigh

(REED hits AUSTIN in the rear with the slapstick and MATT says, "Ow" —all in rhythm with the song.)

AUSTIN: O'er the fields we go

(REED pushes the whoopee cushion)

AUSTIN: Laughing all the way!

(AUSTIN tickles MATT.)

MATT: *(In rhythm)* Ha, ha, ha!

AUSTIN: Bells on bobtails ring

(REED shakes sleigh bells in rhythm.)

AUSTIN: Making spirits bright

(REED blows the party horn.)

AUSTIN: What fun it is to ride and sing
A sleighing song tonight

MATT: Everybody!

(All three guys sing, along with the audience.)

ALL: Jingle Bells
Jingle Bells
Jingle All The Way

(REED blows the duck call.)

ALL: Oh, what fun it is to ride
In a one-horse open sleigh

(*They point to the audience, who yell "Hey!" by themselves.*)

ALL: Jingle Bells
Jingle Bells
Jingle All The Way

(REED *blows the siren whistle.*)

ALL: Oh, what fun it is to ride—

(MATT *and* REED *hold their note as* AUSTIN *speaks. Perhaps they gasp for air somewhere in the middle of* AUSTIN's *speech so they can continue singing the note.*)

AUSTIN: Ladies and gentlemen, we're going to take a break now. But if you bought or brought a gift, put it under the tree and take another present for yourself. We'll be back in fifteen minutes!

(*Then they sing the final line.*)

ALL: In a one-horse open sleigh!

(REED *punctuates the end of the song with another duck call. Blackout*)

END ACT ONE

ACT TWO

(As the intermission music dies down, MATT sneaks on, carrying a gift bag. He checks both doorways to make sure the others aren't around, then places his bag under the tree and picks up a different gift, which he opens.)

MATT: Wow! A hundred dollar gift card—from Borders! Sweet.

(By this time, the stage lights have come up. He notices the audience.)

MATT: Oh hey. Didn't see you there. Y'know, the Ladies' Auxiliary was supposed to do something to start the second act but they couldn't get here. But it got me thinking... Christmas has so many wonderful things going for it, but what it doesn't have is a lot of women. Sure, there's the Virgin Mary, Mother of Jesus. And on the other end of the spectrum, there's Vixen. You know, the reindeer? On Dasher, on Dancer, even on Prancer... You know what I'm talking about. Anyway, that's pretty much it. But there is another gal associated with Christmas, a take-charge kinda lady you don't hear much about. Let's see if we can change that...

(MATT gets a guitar and jumps into a driving Bo Diddley rhythm in G. He sings. [Note: Chords in () are for piano.] A recording of this song, plus sheet music and backing track can be found at https://www.broadwayplaypub.com/the-plays/the-ultimate-christmas-show-abridged/)

MATT:
G (E)
It's pretty calm throughout the year
                    D (B)
Up there at the North Pole
But now it's Christmas Eve
                         G (E)
And it is time to rock and roll
The elves are busy making toys
                    D (B)
The order's pretty large
    D (B)   *Am (Dmb5)*   *Am7 (F#m7)*   *D7 (B7)*
And everybody cowers from the person who's in
charge—
G
Mrs Santa Claus
            D
Mrs Santa Claus
        D   *Am7*
Her ladyship will crack the whip
C/D (A)   *G*
Mrs Santa Claus

(AUSTIN *and* REED *appear and provide oo-wa harmony.*)

MATT:	AUSTIN/REED:
G	**B/D**
She marches through the factory	Ooooooooooooooooooooo
D	**A/D**
A walking cloud of doom	Oooooo Ooo-wa Ooo-wa!
Terrorizing reindeer	**A/D**
G	Ooooooooooooooooooooo
Kicking elves across the room	**B/D**
	Wahh!
D	**B/D**
Now everybody thinks her jolly husband is the boss	Ooooooooooooooooooooo
	A/D
	Oooooo Ooo-wa Ooo-wa!

MATT/REED/AUSTIN:
    D/A/D   *D/A/E*   *D/C/F#*
But who is always sober when Santa hits the sauce?
G/B/D
Mrs Santa Claus
        D/F#
Mrs Santa Claus

MATT: REED/AUSTIN:
    D   *Am7*   **D/F#**   **C/E**
The iron hand behind the   Ooooooo Oooooooo
man

ALL:
C/E   *G/B/D*
Mrs Santa Claus

(The guys chant the next section.)

MATT: Her hair is shiny silver and her cheeks are cherry red

REED: Granny glasses on her nose, a bonnet on her head

AUSTIN: She maps out how to get around the world in just one night

ALL: 'Cause Santa can't find his own butt with both hands and a big flashlight

AUSTIN/REED: *(Spoken)* Key change!

(MATT modulates up a half-step.)

MATT: AUSTIN/REED:
Ab   **C/Eb**
And where is Mr Santa,   Ooo/oooooooooooooooooo
                Eb   **Bb/Eb**
Friend to kids around the   Oooooo Ooo-wa Ooo-wa!
world?

                           Bb/Eb
He's drying out in rehab   Ooooooooooooooooooooo

              Ab   **C/Eb**
With a sixteen year old girl   Oooooo Ooo-wa Ooo-wa!
Though he can hardly stand
up   **C/Eb**

            Eb   Ooooooooooooooooooooo
and his vision is a blur   **Bb/Eb**
                       Oooooo Ooo-wa Ooo-wa!

ALL:
   Eb/Bb/Eb   Bbm/Bb/F
Like all good men before him he'd be nothing without
Eb/Db/G
her...

AUSTIN:
Eb   G
Without her

REED:
G   Bb
Without her

AUSTIN: *(Up an octave)*
Eb   G
Without her

ALL:
Ab/C/Eb
Mrs Santa Claus
       Eb/G
Mrs Santa Claus

MATT: REED/AUSTIN:
Eb   *Bbm7*   **Eb/G**   **Db/F**
The awesome chick behind Ooooooo Ooooooo
Saint Nick

ALL:
Db/F   *C/Eb*
Mrs Santa Claus
Ab/C/Eb

Mrs Santa Claus
   Eb/G
Mrs Santa Claus

MATT: AUSTIN/REED:
Eb   *Eb/G* *Db/F*
When he's off his sleigh, Ooooooo Oooooooo
  Bbm7
she'll save the day!

ALL:
Db/F *Ab—C/Eb*
Mrs Santa Claus

(They slow down.)

ALL:
Bbm—Bb/F *Db—Ab/F*
Every year the children cheer…
Db—Db/F   *Dbm—Db/E* *Ab/Eb/C/Eb*
For Mrs — — — Santa Claus!

(They bow and MATT *runs off to ditch his guitar.)*

AUSTIN: Welcome back, everybody. During intermission Gladys told us that some of the acts scheduled to perform have actually made their connections. So we're crossing our fingers they just might get here. And in the meantime, let's check in on the Christmas gift exchange.

MATT: Goodie, goodie, goodie! *(He re-enters and runs over to the tree to grab a present.)*

REED: Hey!

AUSTIN: Woah woah woah! The gift exchange is for the people who left a present under the tree.

MATT: You're hilarious.

REED: Yes, he is. And he's also serious. Austin?

AUSTIN: *(Snatching the gift away)* Yoink.

MATT: I am so gonna deck your halls. *(He storms off.)*

AUSTIN: Let's see, I'll take this one… *(Spots a larger gift bag; hands it to* REED*)* Oh, do you want this one?

REED: Yes, please!

AUSTIN: *(To the audience)* So how many of you exchanged gifts? What'd you get? Anything good?

*(*AUSTIN *speaks with the audience about the wonderful or lame gifts they've received.)*

AUSTIN: Well, god bless us every—one second! *(Excited, to* REED*)* Since Patrick Stewart can't be here, can I play Scrooge?

REED: It'd be relief for just one Christmas to not have to sit through another *Christmas Carol*.

AUSTIN: Oh, come on. Just a little Dickens?

REED: No.

AUSTIN: *(Opening his present)* Humbug. I totally got Scrooged.

REED: What?!

*(*AUSTIN *holds up the D V D of the Bill Murray classic.)*

AUSTIN: The movie. With Bill Murray. I already have it on Blu-Ray.

REED: Oh. That was from me. You're welcome. It's the thought that counts.

AUSTIN: Yeah. Keep thinking.

*(*AUSTIN *exits.* REED *pulls a fruitcake from his gift bag.)*

REED: *(Reading the label)* "The Official Fruitcake of the 1984 Los Angeles Olympic Games."

*(*MATT *enters wearing a Santa Hat and carrying a bell and red Salvation Army Kettle…except it's spelled "Salivation".)*

MATT: *(Ringing the bell)* Salivation Army! Hi Reed. How about spreading a little Christmas cheer?

REED: Oh absolutely. Here you go. Merry Christmas! *(He drops some coins in the kettle and starts to go.)*

MATT: Thanks, Reed. Happy holidays!

REED: What?

MATT: Happy holidays!

REED: Do you work at Starbucks? How about wishing me a "Merry Christmas'"?

MATT: Reed, not everyone celebrates Christmas, so now we say "Happy Holidays".

REED: But Christmas is about love and joy, and "Happy Holidays"pisses me off!

MATT: Oh, I'm sorry. Happy mid-winter celebration.

REED: Do I look like a pagan to you?

MATT: I don't know. What does a pagan look like?

REED: Like Austin.

MATT: Okay, how about we just be a little forward looking and wish each other a happy January.

REED: How dare you! January is named after the Roman God Janus. Why don't you wish me a Happy March, too, and assume I worship Mars, the Roman God of Candy Bars?

MATT: Okay, what if we wait until January first and wish each other a happy new year?

REED: You sadistic son of a bitch! You know very well I'm Chinese!

MATT: I didn't, but Gung Hay Fat Choy!

REED: Yeah, Gung Hay Fat Choy to the world. Happy holidays.

(REED *starts to exit but realizes he just wished* MATT *"Happy Holidays".* AUSTIN *enters holding three manuscripts.)*

AUSTIN: Hey Reed.

REED: Yeah?

(MATT *rings his bell.)*

MATT: Salivation Army!

AUSTIN: Sure. Here you go! *(He puts money in the kettle and turns to* REED.) Reed, I'm confused.

REED: Yeah, me too. I just wished Matt happy holidays.

AUSTIN: Careful. You can't trust that g—

(They look at MATT, *who's taking the money out of the kettle.)*

AUSTIN/REED: Hey!

MATT: *(Startled)* Uh…Gung Hay Fat Wallet!

(MATT runs off. AUSTIN *looks in the wings.)*

AUSTIN: Anyway—what?

(AUSTIN is handed a slip of paper.)

AUSTIN: Oh, fantastic! *(Reading)* Ladies and gentlemen, "The Muslim-American Ramadancers have just landed at the airport." That's great— *(Unfolding the rest of the note)* "But they're being detained by Homeland Security." Doggone it! *(To the heavens)* Would it kill you to just let one act arrive tonight?

REED: Well Austin, I didn't want to say anything, but maybe if you said a little prayer…?

AUSTIN: I am not gonna pray.

REED: I'm just saying, if you offered up a little *gloria in excelsis deo*, it couldn't hurt.

AUSTIN: I just want one act to go arrive tonight. Is that too much to ask?

REED: I just want an old-fashioned Christmas!

AUSTIN: No you don't.

REED: Why?

AUSTIN: Because an old-fashioned Christmas was totally Pagan.

REED: What?

AUSTIN: Yeah, it was like Mardi Gras combined with the London riots. Why do you think the Puritans tried to ban Christmas?

REED: Where do you get this crap?

AUSTIN: From the Christmas carol lyrics *you* gave me! It's all there. The Holiday Historical Society was supposed to be here to talk about this. In olden days, on the day after Christmas, mobs of poor people in England used to storm the homes of rich people and threaten them if they didn't give them food. They would put the food in boxes, that's why the Brits call it Boxing Day. You know that song "We Wish You a Merry Christmas"?

REED: I love that song!

AUSTIN: Well, that's what that Christmas carol is all about— *(Singing)*
Now give us some figgy pudding

(MATT *runs on and joins in. They do the storming-the-barricades choreography from Les Miz as they sing and back* REED *up against the Christmas tree.*)

AUSTIN/MATT: *(Singing)*
Now give us some figgy pudding
Now give us some figgy pudding
And give it right now!

REED: My god.

AUSTIN/MATT: *(Singing)*
We won't go until we get some
We won't go until we get some
We won't go until we get some

MATT: *(Singing)*
Or we'll eat your cow!

AUSTIN: How do you like your old-fashioned Christmas now, guv'nor?

REED: Not much. So how did we get the Christmas I love?

MATT: Well, Reed, you're not gonna want to hear this—

REED: Oh come on. I can take it.

MATT: Well—Christmas was saved by Santa Claus.

(REED *breaks through them and crosses to the other side of the stage.*)

REED: No!

MATT: Calm down! Take a breath!

REED: I don't want to hear about that guy.

AUSTIN: What is wrong with you?

REED: I hate Santa.

MATT: You do not.

REED: Yes I do.

AUSTIN: Come on, Reed. Santa's awesome! You know why he's so jolly, don't you?

REED: No.

AUSTIN: 'Cause he knows where all the naughty girls live.

(AUSTIN *and* MATT *high-five.*)

REED: Yeah, it's all a big joke to you but I can't help it. I just—when I was a kid I used to have this recurring nightmare: Santa was like Big Brother. He'd see me when I was sleeping. He'd know when I was awake. He'd know if I'd been bad or good.

AUSTIN: Oh grow up for goodness' sake.

MATT: So—you're afraid of Santa Claus.

REED: *(Quiet; serious)* Yes! I have Santa Claustrophobia.

MATT: Reed, you should love Santa. He saved Christmas!

REED: Stop saying that!

AUSTIN/MATT: But it's true.

MATT: Before Santa was popularized by the poem *The Night Before Christmas* in 1822, churches were closed on Christmas because the celebrations were too dangerous and too pagan.

AUSTIN: But then, after that poem, Santa was everywhere! On posters, in advertising, in stores. Suddenly Christmas was safe and wholesome. People figured out that instead of drunken riots, Christmas could be about love, and family, and giving—

MATT: And getting—

AUSTIN: And that's when families—and churches—began to celebrate Christmas the way you know and love it. I know it's a cliche to say commercialization has ruined Christmas but actually, when you think about it, commercialization *saved* Christmas.

(REED takes this in, then quietly exits.)

MATT: Where's he going?

AUSTIN: It's a lot to process.

MATT: Yeah. For Reed's sake, I'm glad Santa couldn't get here tonight, but I wanted to ask him about my wish list. You know what, I'm gonna call his 800 number.

AUSTIN: Whose 800 number?

MATT: 1-800-SANTA. Don't worry, I'll put it on speaker.

(*Over the speakers, we hear the noise of dialing, ringing, and the click of someone answering.*)

AUSTIN: 1-800-SANTA?

MATT: Yeah, I found it online…

(*Suddenly we hear* REED *speaking on an offstage microphone. In an Indian accent.*)

REED/SANTA: (*O S*) Ho, ho, ho. 1-800-SANTA. This is Sanjay Claus.

(*Beat*)

MATT: Where are you from?

REED/SANTA: (*O S*) Oh, I am from the North Pole.

MATT: You have a very unusual accent.

REED/SANTA: (*O S*) That's the way everyone talks up here.

AUSTIN: Hey Santa, Austin Tichenor here…

REED/SANTA: (*O S*) Oh I have very bad news for you, Austin Tichenor.

AUSTIN: What's that?

REED/SANTA: (*O S*) No presents for non-believing Pagans.

AUSTIN: I'm not a pagan!

(AUSTIN *crosses away. During this next dialogue, he notices the Christmas tree lights aren't on. He follows the extension cord into the wings, discovers it's not plugged in, then finds an outlet on the proscenium or on the floor near the tree. He plugs it in, but the lights still don't come on.*)

MATT: Hi Santa, Matt Rippy here. Long-time believer, first-time caller.

REED/SANTA: *(O S)* Yes, Matt Rippy. What would you like Sanjay to get you for Christmas?

MATT: I was hoping you could bring me some candy.

REED/SANTA: *(O S)* Oh, I have lots of candy. Mahatma Candy, Indira Candy…

MATT: But what I really want is a Harley.

REED/SANTA: *(O S)* Harley Krishna or Harley Rama?

MATT: Harley Davidson. Its rubber-mounted V-twin engine really sings.

REED/SANTA: *(O S)* Oh, we love to sing here at the North Pole. *(Singing)*
Deck the Taj Mahal with Hari Krishnu
Fa la la la la, la la la la
Get on your knees and pray to Vishnu
Fa la la la la, la la la la
Find a yoga pose to suit ya'
Fa la la la la, la la la la
Bend we now for Kama Sutra
Fa la la la la, la la la la
(Spoken) Happy Nehru, everybody! Have I provided you with excellent service today, Matt Rippy?

(During this, AUSTIN *hears the singing and rejoins* MATT.*)*

MATT: Yeah, you've been great, thanks.

REED/SANTA: Good bye, Matt Rippy. Good bye, pagan!

MATT: Goodbye. Sanjay Claus, everybody! *(Hanging up)* Wow. Even Santa's been outsourced.

*(*MATT *exits.* AUSTIN *walks with him until he sees* REED *entering.)*

AUSTIN: Well, it was just a matter of—hey. You okay?

REED: Yeah, I had a phone call. I know I should broaden my perspective on Christmas, but I don't know how.

AUSTIN: I know. Obviously this is all very new to you, and very confusing. But I had a thought... *(Suddenly singing a cappella)*

C
It came to me on a midnight clear...

REED: What did?

AUSTIN: *(Putting a finger to* REED*'s lips)* Shh! *(Singing)*

  Dm7   G7
There's so much confusion these days...

REED: Why are you singing?

AUSTIN: Reed, everybody sings at Christmas! *(Singing)*

 C
To make things easy this time of year

  Dm7   G7
Just learn to say one simple phrase...

REED: *(Hopefully)* Merry Christmas!

AUSTIN: Close. *(Singing)*

C
Happy Merry Chrismakwanukkahanzukkah

       G7
That's the only thing you'll ever have to say

     C
Happy Merry Chrismakwanukkahanzukkah

  Dm7   G7
Wishes everyone a jolly holiday!

C
Happy Merry Chrismakwanukkahanzukkah

    F   Bb
If you wanna spread some universal cheer, say

G7 C   A
Happy Merry Chrismakwanukkahanzukkah

   Dm7   G

You know you wannakah
    C
This year!
(He finishes with a big ta-da.)

REED: Thank you. I'll try to keep that in mind.

AUSTIN: I know you will. Oh, I have another big surprise for you...

(AUSTIN presents the three manuscripts with a flourish and REED takes one.)

AUSTIN: Your traditional English Christmas Panto, m'lord.

REED: Really? I love Christmas Pantomimes!

AUSTIN: I know you do. Matt? Ah!

(MATT has entered and is right behind him. AUSTIN hands a script to him.)

REED: Whenever I'm in London over the holidays I make sure I see one. Has anyone here ever seen a Panto? Don't worry, whether you have or not, you're gonna love it. Pantos are irreverent and slightly bawdy...

AUSTIN: And there's always a B-list celebrity in the cast...

MATT: And every panto has a man of a certain age playing a woman.

AUSTIN: And there's always an evil villain...

REED: Is there any other kind?

AUSTIN: No, you're right. Love the villains!

REED: And the actors always end up playing animals.

MATT: And no Christmas panto would be complete without candy being tossed into the audience. *(He pulls a handful of small candies from his pocket and starts to throw them to the crowd, but stops.)* Ooh, Snickers Minis!

REED: So which story are we doing?

AUSTIN: Ah! We are going to do the traditional Christmas panto.

REED: Yeah, which one?

AUSTIN: What do you mean which one? Doesn't every Christmas panto tell the story of the first Christmas?

REED: No, that would be disrespectful.

AUSTIN: Why?

REED: Because they're irreverent and slightly bawdy! A panto tells a children's story like *Jack and the Bean Stalk* or *Cinderella* or *Aladdin* or …

AUSTIN: Shouldn't a Christmas panto tell the story of Jesus?

REED: No! Pantos are based on fairy tales!

AUSTIN: Like Jesus! Perfect!

REED: Stop it!

(*Lighting. Thunder. The lights dim momentarily. This storm's worse than the previous two.*)

REED: (*To* AUSTIN) See what you did!

(AUSTIN *points to a guy in the audience.*)

AUSTIN: He did it.

MATT: Woah, we gotta hurry.

AUSTIN: That storm's getting closer! (*He runs off.*)

REED: (*Flipping through the pages*) We can't tell the story of Jesus like *this*. We need something else.

AUSTIN: (*O S*) There's no time!

REED: (*To* MATT) We should do the panto first then *finish* with the Nativity story.

MATT: We'll do both at the same time. We gotta get these people outa here before they close the roads. Let's go!

(MATT *pushes* REED *offstage and turns to the audience.*)

MATT: *(To the audience)* Ladies and gentlemen, the Saint Everybody's Ensemble is now proud to present a traditional English Panto that will, for what is apparently the first time ever, really be a *Christmas Panto*. Lights!

(Blackout. Holiday Music. A light comes up on Austin dressed in a T V reporter's blazer and fake white beard.)

AUSTIN/WOLF BLITZEN: Good evening, ladies and gentlemen, boys and girls. From C N N, the Christmas News Network, I'm B-list celebrity Wolf Blitzen. I'm here to tell you the story of the Very First Christmas! Are you excited for the story to begin?

(The audience responds lamely.)

AUSTIN/WOLF BLITZEN: Oh you're going to have to do better than that! Are you excited for the story to begin?

(Better response)

AUSTIN/WOLF BLITZEN: Much better! Now, the first thing you have to do is, if somebody's behind us, you have to yell out, "He's behind you!" For instance, Matt Rippy is going to be in this Panto. Where is he?

(MATT sneaks on and hides behind AUSTIN. The audience yells "He's behind you!")

AUSTIN/WOLF BLITZEN: Very good! It's adorable how stupid that is.

MATT: Yes it is. *(He exits.)*

AUSTIN/WOLF BLITZEN: And if one of the characters says, "Oh no it isn't!" You have to say, "Oh yes it is!" And you have to boo the bad guy, just boo and hiss like crazy the minute the bad guy appears.

(REED *walks onstage, flipping through his script.*)

REED: Hey Austin—

(The audience hisses and boos.)

REED: Hey, I'm not the bad guy!

AUSTIN/WOLF BLITZEN: Well, not in the Panto but—
(To the audience) Great energy, though.

REED: Why aren't I playing the baby Jesus? 'Cause, you know, that's my whole thing—

AUSTIN/WOLF BLITZEN: *(Pushing REED off)* Yeah, I know. Don't worry, Reed. I got something even better planned for you. Just read farther along in the script. It's all taken care of. Everything's kosher. *(To the audience)* So! Ladies and gentlemen, I think we're ready now to tell the story of the first Christmas. Let's go back to the very beginning. It all started with a beautiful young lady played by a man of a certain age.

(AUSTIN *leaves.* REED *enters, reluctantly, dressed as* MARY *with a big pregnancy bump.*)

REED/MARY: *(To audience)* You are *not* going to believe what happened. The angel of the Lord visited me and told me that I was going to have a baby who would be the savior of the world. And I said that because I have not yet been with Joseph, that's impossible. And the angel said…

(MATT *enters as* CLARENCE, *with cheap halo and no wings.*)

MATT/CLARENCE: "Oh no it isn't!"

REED/MARY: *(Encouraging the audience to join in)* "Oh, yes it is!"

MATT/CLARENCE: "Oh no it isn't!"

REED/MARY: "Oh, yes, it is!"

(They react to the audience's reaction.)

REED/MARY: But I can't be having a baby. It's impossible.

MATT/CLARENCE: Nothing is impossible with God. And if you have this baby, he will be the Messiah—the savior of the world. But much more importantly, I'll get my wings. Don't worry about Joseph. *(He exits.)*

REED/MARY: Oh I am worried about many things, but not about Joseph. He is the most gentle, kind, soft-spoken—

(AUSTIN enters as JOSEPH.)

AUSTIN/JOSEPH: *(Yelling)* You're *what?*

REED/MARY: You heard me.

AUSTIN/JOSEPH: But I saw you yesterday and you didn't have a bump. How could this happen so quickly?

REED/MARY: Because we've only got twenty-five minutes left in the show.

AUSTIN/JOSEPH: Right.

REED/MARY: Joseph, it's a miracle.

AUSTIN/JOSEPH: I thought I was the only man for you.

REED/MARY: He was an angel!

AUSTIN/JOSEPH: Well, clearly he was very, very charming.

REED/MARY: No, he was literally an angel. Clarence told me I was going to have a baby that would save the world from its sin.

AUSTIN/JOSEPH: I can't believe you fell for that old line. I feel like breaking it off.

REED/MARY: Wouldn't that hurt?

AUSTIN/JOSEPH: What are you talking about?

REED/MARY: What are *you* talking about?

AUSTIN/JOSEPH: Breaking off our engagement.

REED/MARY: Oh! I thought you meant…

AUSTIN/JOSEPH: What has gotten into you?

(They both look at MARY's *bump).*

AUSTIN/JOSEPH: I mean, what is *wrong* with you?

REED/MARY: Well, for one thing I'm pregnant and not married.

AUSTIN/JOSEPH: Oh, don't worry about that. I'll marry you.

REED/MARY: *(Taking his arm)* Oh, Joseph, you are a good man.

AUSTIN/JOSEPH: Yes, but I'm hard to find.

(They exit. WOLF BLITZEN *appears again—but this time played by* MATT. *He struggles to get his beard on properly.)*

MATT/WOLF BLITZEN: Hello, now *I'm* B-list celebrity Wolf Blitzen. Every Christmas panto has a villain and ours is a real baddie. When the King of Judea heard that a new king was about to born, he decided to do something about it. You know what to do when you see an evil villain. Ladies and gentlemen, I give you the evil & nasty King Herod of Judea!

*(*MATT *exits.* AUSTIN *enters as* HEROD. *He uses his Scroogiest voice and scowls at the audience when they "boo" him.)*

AUSTIN/HEROD: Humbug! May a rabid camel hump your grandmother! Three wise men have told me a new king is about to be born. Can I let this happen?

(NOTE: Sometimes there's little response here, but most times the audience will answer "No" first, then rethink and start saying "Yes". If that happens, preface the next line with "You were right the first time. Don't over-think it!")

AUSTIN/HEROD: The answer is "No", you imbeciles! These "astrologers" say they must follow a star to find this child king. I must get them to help me rid the world of this newborn baby.

(AUSTIN/HEROD *laughs evilly at the audience in the middle of the theatre, then runs stage-right and laughs at that side, then runs all the way left and laughs at that side. The audience will 'boo' him vigorously. All that running and evil laughing leaves him winded.*)

AUSTIN/HEROD: Aw, nuts. I need my three wise men! Wise Men! Get in here!

(MATT *and* REED *enter as* MELCHIOR *and* BALTHAZAR, *dressed in crazy matching '70s disco outfits.*)

AUSTIN/HEROD: I'm sorry. Did I interrupt disco night?

MATT/MELCHIOR: Sorry, your highness. The costume trunks didn't arrive.

REED/BALTHAZAR: These are the only matching outfits we could find.

AUSTIN/HEROD: I was expecting Balthazar, Melchior, and Caspar. There's supposed to be *three* wise men.

REED/BALTHAZAR: Yeah, but you're supposed to be the thir—

AUSTIN: *(Cutting him off)* Uh, uh, uh!

REED/BALTHAZAR: Uh, Caspar's on his way.

AUSTIN/HEROD: Really. Will he be played by a devilishly talented thespian?

MATT/MELCHIOR: Well, you do like women, so…

AUSTIN/HEROD: *Thespian*, you imbecile! Not a lesbi— never mind. Go get me the third astrologer!

MATT/MELCHIOR: Okay… *(He exits.)*

REED/BALTHAZAR: I'm sorry about this, your highness. *(Calling to offstage actor)* Caspar, get in here!

(MATT *enters, covered in a white sheet. He makes ghostly noises and moves spookily.*)

AUSTIN/HEROD: Don't tell me. You're Caspar.

MATT/CASPAR: *(In a phony, deep ghost voice)* Yes, the Friendly Astrologer.

AUSTIN/HEROD: You're just Melchior in a white sheet.

MATT/CASPAR: No, no, no.

AUSTIN/HEROD: Yes, yes, yes. Where's Melchior?

MATT/CASPAR: He's behind you!

AUSTIN/HEROD: Nice try. Go get me the third astrologer.

MATT/CASPAR: *(Exiting)* Oooooh...kay.

AUSTIN/HEROD: I specifically ordered three wise men, not two total idiots!

(MATT *enters as* MELCHIOR *again.*)

MATT/MELCHIOR: You called?

AUSTIN/HEROD: Speak of the devil.

MATT/MELCHIOR: What do you need?

AUSTIN/HEROD: I need you and Caspar here at the same time!

REED/BALTHAZAR: I'll get him, your highness. *(He exits.)*

AUSTIN/HEROD: Thank you! Finally! Now we're getting somewhere.

(Now REED *enters wearing the sheet. He does a series of Three Stooges noises and moves, ending with a sepulchral "Luke, I am your father.")*

AUSTIN/HEROD: I don't understand—are you Darth Curly? Are you finished?

REED/CASPAR: My career is.

(HEROD *rips the sheet off* BALTHAZAR.)

AUSTIN/HEROD: *(Furious)* I need you two to stop goofing around! And I need you to find that baby and report his whereabouts to me so that I can, I can...! *(Realizing he's revealing his plan, suddenly calm and friendly)* ...send him some lovely prezzies for his baby shower.

MATT/MELCHIOR: Do you plan to harm the child?

AUSTIN/HEROD: No, no. I *love* children. I love them to death! Now off with you. Find me that baby. Have a good trip. Hurry back! Look both ways before crossing the Sinai! T T F N! L O L! F U!

(AUSTIN/HEROD *laughs evilly as* MELCHIOR *and* BALTHAZAR *exit. The audience boos.*

AUSTIN/HEROD: *(To the audience)* What? I *do* love children—especially with a little gravy and a side of mashed potatoes!

(AUSTIN/HEROD *laughs evilly and exits.* MATT *as* WOLF BLITZEN *enters.)*

MATT/WOLF BLITZEN: Ooh, he's so nasty! And so overacting! Meanwhile, Mary and Joseph were traveling to Bethlehem because all Roman subjects had to return to their hometowns for a census. This made finding a hotel extremely difficult, but Mary, even in her heavily pregnant state, was already displaying the patience of the saint she would eventually become.

(MATT *exits as* MARY *enters, the long-suffering* JOSEPH *following.)*

REED/MARY: *(Irritable)* Jesus Christ! I *told* you to make reservations, but you wouldn't listen!

AUSTIN/JOSEPH: Darling, love of my life, we've been through this. I tried to call but my cell phone won't get reception for another two thousand years.

REED/MARY: And not even then if you have AT&T. Let's try this place. Hello?

(MATT *appears as an air-headed hotel* CLERK.)

MATT/CLERK: Good evening. May I help you? *(Sees the bump)* Woah, it looks like you've already been helped.

REED/MARY: Watch it!

AUSTIN/JOSEPH: Do you have a room?

MATT/CLERK: Sorry. We're totally full.

REED/MARY: *(Panting)* But we really need a room. I'm going to have a baby any minute!

MATT/CLERK: I'm afraid it's out of my hands.

REED/MARY: It's gonna be *in* your hands in a minute. *(A big contraction hits* MARY.*)* Woah! My water's breaking!

MATT/CLERK: Oh no it isn't.

REED/MARY: *(Encouraging the audience to join in, which they always do)* Oh yes it is!

MATT/CLERK: Oh no it isn't!

REED/MARY: Oh yes it is! I'm having this baby— *(Like a possessed Linda Blair, he grabs the* CLERK *by the shirt)* — right now!! Aah!

MATT/CLERK: Aah!

AUSTIN/JOSEPH: Aah!

MATT/CLERK: There's a stable 'round back. Take it! Take it! *(He runs out.)*

AUSTIN/JOSEPH: Are you okay?

REED/MARY: *(Suddenly completely calm)* Oh, yeah. I was faking.

AUSTIN/JOSEPH: Ah, Mary, for a saint you've got a bit of the devil in ya.

(They high-five and exit. MATT *enters as* WOLF BLITZEN.*)*

MATT/WOLF BLITZEN: Meanwhile— *(Unfortunately, although he's remembered the blazer, he's forgotten the beard. He steps off then immediately returns wearing it.)* Meanwhile, under orders from the *evil King Herod…* *(He loads the name, prompting boos.)* The three wise men were following the Star of Bethlehem, trying to find this newborn King of the Jews.

*(*AUSTIN *enters wearing the Wise Men disco outfit.)*

AUSTIN/CASPAR: "Where is He who has been born King of the Jews? For we have seen His star in the East and have come to worship Him." *(Cockily, to the audience)* Matthew 2:2. *(Realizing he's alone)* Balthazar, Melchior! Keep up! We must worship the Christ child.

*(*MATT *and* REED *enter wearing the matching disco outfits. They're out of character and unhappy.)*

AUSTIN/CASPAR: *(Spurring them on)* Don't worry, I'm following the Star of Bethlehem—on Twitter!

MATT: I still don't see why we have to wear these stupid costumes.

AUSTIN: Come on, we look fabulous. This Bee Gees look is really coming back.

MATT: Why are we even here? We bring the Christ-child presents and then completely disappear from the story.

REED: Yeah, people will probably forget all about us.

AUSTIN/CASPAR: Forget all about us? Are you crazy? Who is fabled in song and story? We three kings of Orient are!

(They all get the same idea at the same time, and start singing a cappella in tight high Bee Gees harmonies. Perhaps there's a sound cue to give them the first note. They do some disco dance moves as they sing.)

ALL: *(To the tune of* Stayin' Alive*)*
We three kings of orient are
Orient are
Bearing gifts we traveled so far-rre
(To the tune of Too Much Heaven*)*
Because nobody gets too much Christmas no more
It's all 'Happy Holidays' and Hanukkah too...
(To the tune of Jive Talkin'*)*
But now it's Christ talkin'
We're tellin' no lies
K-K-K-Christ talkin'
In our Bee Gees disguise!
(To the tune of You Should Be Dancing*)*
And now it's Christmas, yeah!

(Blackout. At the peak of the applause, we hear pre-recorded animal noises. Lights up on the three actors kneeling on all fours: AUSTIN *dressed as a pig,* REED *as a cow, and* MATT *as a sheep.)*

AUSTIN/PIG: I can't believe they kicked us out of our own stable.

MATT/SHEEP: Yeah, who do they think they are?

REED/COW: Give them a break! She's about to go into labor. Besides, it's an honor to allow our home to be the birthplace of the most important person in history.

MATT/SHEEP: That woman is giving birth to *[2011]* Lady Gaga *[2012]* Justin Bieber?

REED/COW: No, she's giving birth to the king of the Jews.

AUSTIN/PIG: Oh, great. That means they're probably going to have one of those big Jewish feasts.

REED/COW: *(To* MATT*)* That means you might get eaten.

MATT/SHEEP: *(To* REED*)* And you might get eaten.

(They both look at the PIG.*)*

REED/COW: *(To* AUSTIN*)* And you—are the luckiest animal I know.

AUSTIN/PIG: I want to go back to my stable. How will we know when it's over? Will there be a sign?

(Heavenly music plays. A bright heavenly light shines on them from the wings.)

REED/COW: I think that might be it.

MATT/SHEEP: Dibs on the placenta!

(He runs off towards the light. AUSTIN *and* REED *exit slowly.)*

REED/COW: Hey, did you get a load of that donkey Mary rode in on?

AUSTIN/PIG: Yeah. Nice ass.

*(*MATT *as* WOLF BLITZEN *enters, barely getting his beard on; in fact, it may be on inside out.)*

MATT/WOLF BLITZEN: We're now getting word from T M Z, *Enlightenment Tonight,* and *Access Holy Rood* that unto us is born this day in the City of David a savior, which is Christ the Lord. Early reports indicate he was attended by his stepfather, a few shepherds, some displaced barnyard animals, the Bee Gees, two turtle doves, and a partridge carrying *(The funniest audience contribution from the* Twelve Days of Christmas *song in* ACT ONE*).*

*(*AUSTIN *has entered upstage as* HEROD.*)*

MATT/WOLF BLITZEN: But so far, no sign of the evil King Herod, right?

(The audience reacts.)

MATT/WOLF BLITZEN: Where?

(The audience reacts again. MATT *looks around, but* AUSTIN *keeps moving out of his eye line.)*

MATT/WOLF BLITZEN: I don't see him. Where is he?

AUDIENCE: He's behind you!

(MATT *looks over his other shoulder and sees* HEROD.)

MATT/WOLF BLITZEN: Aha! Get out of here! This is my scene!

AUSTIN/HEROD: Damn you, B-list celebrity Wolf Blitzen! May visions of Ann Coulter *(Or another annoying celebrity in the news)* dance in your head! Ugh, I just threw up in my mouth a little… *(He exits.)*

MATT/WOLF BLITZEN: *(To audience)* Anyway, as I was saying, early reports indicate that the Holy Family was inundated by visitors. *(Realizing)* But then, because the three actors realized…we can't play both the Holy Family *and* all the visitors who attended the manger…

(AUSTIN *has stepped onstage, flipping through the script and coming to the same realization.* MATT *crosses to him and they confer for less than a second.*)

MATT/WOLF BLITZEN: —they decided they should go into the audience to pick out three volunteers.

(AUSTIN *enters holding three robes. He and* MATT *look out into the audience to see who they should pick to play the Holy Family—*)

(*—as* REED *enters wearing absolutely nothing except a huge swaddling diaper and baby bonnet. He thinks he's going to help pick out volunteers too.*)

REED: So let's see, I'll play baby Jesus. Maybe she can play Mary and he can play…

MATT: Reed! What are you wearing?

REED: Hey, if anyone's playing the Baby Jesus, *I'm* playing the Baby Jesus!

MATT: C'mon, Reed, let's get you dressed, you're scaring the front row.

(MATT *leads* REED *offstage.*)

AUSTIN: *(To the audience)* Forgive him. He knows not what he does. Um, could I get some house lights please? We just need a holy family. Is there a particularly holy family out here we can borrow? Now, we want this to be an historically accurate Christmas pageant. Do we have any Jews?

(AUSTIN *grabs three audience members and brings them onstage. He dresses them as Mary, Joseph and the baby Jesus.*)

AUSTIN: Here, put this on and look kind of useless. You'll be Joseph. You put this on and play Mary—I assume you're a virgin. And you put this on and play Jesus. Hey, you look divine! Now all you gotta do is just stand there and act holier than— *(Re: the audience)* —them. The Holy Family, everybody!

(AUSTIN *exits as we hear a swing version of "Away In A Manger". The guys re-enter as the Angels.* MATT *is dressed as* CLARENCE *but now wears wings.* AUSTIN *has a white robe and wings and carries a long horn.* REED *wears a Los Angeles Angels shirt and cap and carries a baseball bat.*)

MATT/CLARENCE: The angels are here to adore the Christ child. I'm Clarence.

AUSTIN/GABRIEL: I'm Gabriel.

REED/LOS ANGELES ANGEL: I'm Albert Pujols. *(Or Mike Trout. Or whoever is the most well-known Los Angeles Angels player at the moment)*

MATT/CLARENCE: Are *you* the baby Jesus? *(To Mary)* It must have been a very difficult birth. Hey look, Mary, I got my wings.

(AUSTIN/GABRIEL *blows his horn.*)

MATT/CLARENCE: Sshh! The baby's asleep!

AUSTIN/GABRIEL: No, he's not.

MATT/CLARENCE: Well, he was asleep the whole first act.

AUSTIN/GABRIEL: So what are we supposed to do?

MATT/CLARENCE: Adore the baby.

(They run up as close as they can to the guy or gal playing the baby Jesus and stare at him/her for a little longer than is comfortable.)

ALL: Ahhhhh…

(MATT gently pinches the Baby Jesus's cheek.)

MATT/CLARENCE: Yep, he's adorable.

ALL: Congratulations!

MATT/CLARENCE: Let's go!

AUSTIN/GABRIEL: Bye! Just hang there for a minute.

(They exit as the swing version of Away In A Manger *plays again, a little faster this time. The music fades as they re-enter.)*

(All three wear shepherd robes. AUSTIN and REED have typical shepherd head wear. MATT wears a German alpine hat. They act as if they're freezing.)

AUSTIN/LEAD SHEPHERD: Can we come in?

REED/ASSISTANT SHEPHERD: It's freezing out there.

AUSTIN/LEAD SHEPHERD: How rude of us. We haven't introduced ourselves. I'm the lead shepherd.

REED/ASSISTANT SHEPHERD: I'm the assistant shepherd.

MATT/GERMAN SHEPHERD: Und I'm ze German Shepherd.

AUSTIN/LEAD SHEPHERD: Two angels and a baseball player appeared to us and said the savior of the world was born tonight. So let's adore the baby.

(The guys adore the baby Jesus as before.)

ALL: Ahhhhh…

MATT/GERMAN SHEPHERD: Ya, he izz adorable.

ALL: Congratulations.

MATT/GERMAN SHEPHERD: Let's go. Auf wiedersehen.

(The SHEPHERDS *exit and* Away In A Manger *plays again, even faster. Now the three guys enter as the animals.* AUSTIN *holds a birthday cake.)*

REED/COW: Well, well, well. Whoooo do we have here?

MATT/SHEEP: It's the baaay-beeee.

AUSTIN/PIG: Hey, Baby Jesus, we brought you a birthday cake.

ALL: *(Singing)*
For you're a jolly good savior
For you're a jolly good savior
For you're a jolly good savior
Who Peter will deny!

REED/COW: Let's adore the baby.

(They adore the baby Jesus as before.)

ALL: Ahhhhh…

MATT/SHEEP: Yep, he's adorable.

ALL: Congratulations.

MATT/SHEEP: Let's go. Laaaay-ter!

REED/COW: Moo-ve!

(They run off, AUSTIN *exiting last and telling the family "It's almost over." Once again we hear the swing music, now irresponsibly fast. The music fades as the Wise Men enter.)*

MATT/MELCHIOR: At last we have reached the holy family! Wise Men, keep up! You are wise, but slow. I am Melchior. I have brought you a gift of gold.

REED/BALTHAZAR: I am Balthazar. I have brought you the gift of frankincense.

AUSTIN/CASPAR: And I am Caspar. I am regifting you this D V D of *Scrooged*.

(They each put their gifts off to the side. Suddenly, AUSTIN/ CASPAR gets an idea.)

MATT/SHEEP: *(To the tune of* Nights on Broadway*)*
Here we are, in a room with a manger

(The others join in.)

ALL: *(Singing)*
Standing in the dark, and we could not look stranger
Well, we came to follow you

(They each step next to one of the audience volunteers, moving them as necessary.)

ALL: To worship the King of the Jews
And we won't stop our loving you
We wont go away

(The three Wise Men do Bee Gees moves in time to the music, and encourage the audience volunteers to join in.)

ALL: *(To the tune of* Night Fever*)*
Silent night fever, night fever
We know how to sing it
Silent night fever, night fever
Even though we wing it

Silent night fever, night fever
We know how to sing it
Silent night fever, night fever
Even though we wing it
(Big finish, to the tune of You Should Be Dancing*)*
And now it's Christmas, yeah!

AUSTIN/CASPAR: Now, we must warn you. You three are in terrible danger. The *evil King Herod…*

(The audiences reacts.)

AUSTIN/CASPAR: ...wants to kill the baby Jesus. You should flee the country until times are safer.

MATT/MELCHIOR: In fact, you should flee in disguise. You should change—*into clothing of the future!* Take off those robes.

(The volunteers remove the robes. AUSTIN *takes the costumes offstage.)*

MATT/MELCHIOR: Yes! Believe it or not, in the future this is what some people will actually wear to the theatre.

REED/BALTHAZAR: Very good. And now—*you must escape into Egypt!* (Indicating their seats) I think it's just down those steps and back to your seats. How about a hand for the Holy Family!

(The volunteers return to their seats. AUSTIN *re-enters.)*

AUSTIN/CASPAR: And now we three must return to the East by a roundabout way so we aren't discovered by the evil King Herod.

(The audience boos on its own and the Wise Men give them a thumbs up.)

AUSTIN/CASPAR: I'm getting drunk from all the boos. Come, let us away!

MATT/MELCHIOR: Wait! We forgot to give Jesus his stocking stuffers.

REED/BALTHAZAR: That's right.

(They reach into their pockets.)

REED/BALTHAZAR: Bubble gum.

MATT/MELCHIOR: Candy.

AUSTIN/CASPAR: And dental floss.

MATT/MELCHIOR: Dude, don't be that guy.

(We hear the sound of an airplane flying overhead. The guys look up.)

ALL: Oh no…

REED/BALTHAZAR: It's Joseph and Mary's flight into Egypt. Now we'll never be able to give the baby his stocking stuffers.

AUSTIN/CASPAR: But if we give them unto these… *(Indicating the audience)* …the least of his brethren, we will have given them unto him.

REED/BALTHAZAR: You're right! Here it comes, folks!

(They toss their treats into the audience.)

REED/BALTHAZAR: Big finish!

ALL: *(To the tune of* You Should Be Dancing. *Finishing with big disco pose)*
And now it's Christmas, yeah!

(Blackout. Lights up on AUSTIN *as* HEROD. *The audience boos as he enters.)*

AUSTIN/HEROD: Humbug! May a particularly aggressive nutcracker fall down your trousers! It's been months since I've seen those Wise Men. They've out-smarted me. But I'll still get that baby! Nobody's ever going to be King of the Jews except for me! Ha, ha, ha! Ha, ha, ha! Ha—

*(*MATT *enters as* WOLF BLITZEN.*)*

MATT/WOLF BLITZEN: Then King Herod dropped dead.

*(*AUSTIN/HEROD *falls to the ground.)*

MATT/WOLF BLITZEN: And the audience was well-pleased.

*(*AUSTIN/HEROD *sits up and struggles into a kneeling position.)*

AUSTIN/HEROD: But wait, B-list celebrity Wolf Blitzen! Does this Christmas Panto tell the story of what did happen or what *might* have happened?

MATT/WOLF BLITZEN: What do you mean?

AUSTIN/HEROD: I am a changed man. From now on, no one will celebrate Jesus's birth more joyously than I! *(He pathetically pleads for sympathy.)*

MATT/WOLF BLITZEN: Oh, what the heck. In this version, King Herod gets a second chance.

(The heavenly light glows from the wings again, with the same music.)

AUSTIN/HEROD: Oh! I am suffused by a heavenly light! I'm glowing! It's the Holy Spirit! Thank you, Spirit! You did it all in one night! *(Singing)* Happy Merry Chrismakwanukkahanzukkah... *(Spoken)* Eat my shorts, Patrick Stewart! *(Starts to laugh evilly)* I mean... *(He laughs delightfully, and skips off.)*

MATT/WOLF BLITZEN: And King Herod's heart grew three sizes that day. The birth of the baby Jesus gave the whole world a reason to celebrate. And nobody was happier than—his mom.

(REED enters again as MARY, now with no pregnancy bump.)

REED/MARY: I am so proud. I know every Jewish mother thinks her boy is the Son of God but mine actually is! And I know people argue about whether it's more important how Jesus was born or how he died...but really, what's most important was how he *lived*. And what I love about Christmas is that it's when people can try to act for one day a year the way my son lived his whole life. *(Some of this begins to hit home. He slowly drops the character.)* And really, it has been going on since the beginning of time, hasn't it? Long before the birth of Jesus, people of all cultures—and religions—gathered in the coldest, darkest time of the year with faith and hope for warmer, brighter days ahead.

(Changed, REED *starts to exit. But* MATT *enters.)*

MATT: Okay guys. Time for presents.

AUSTIN: *(Entering)* We don't have anything for you.

MATT: That's okay. These are for you.

*(*MATT *hands both* AUSTIN *and* REED *a beautifully wrapped gift.)*

REED: Wow.

AUSTIN: But we didn't get you anything.

MATT: I'm good.

*(*MATT *exits, and* REED *starts to follow.* AUSTIN, *moved by what he's seen, starts to sing.* MATT *and* REED *are very pleasantly surprised.)*

AUSTIN: *(Singing)*

Angels we have heard on high
Sweetly singing o'er the plains

*(*MATT *returns as* REED *joins in.)*

AUSTIN/REED: *(Singing)*
And the mountains in reply

(Now MATT *joins in.)*

ALL: *(Singing)*
Echoing their joyful strains
Glo-o-o-o-o-ria
In egg shell seas deo

AUSTIN: Day-o!

*(*REED *shoots* AUSTIN *a look.* AUSTIN *agrees that was too much and they all gesture for the audience to join in.)*

ALL: Glo-o-o-o-o-ria
In egg shell seas day-hey-yo!

(Slow fade to black. The lights come up. The guys look at each other, wondering what to do next. AUSTIN *wanders to the wing.)*

MATT: Ladies and gentlemen, that's about as much of the Multicultural Interfaith Holiday Variety Show and Christmas Pageant as we can do tonight.

REED: We don't know if the roads are clear yet, so we all may need to hang here for a little bit.

AUSTIN: *(Re-entering, laughing)* Knock it off, Gladys, I am *not* gonna fall for that again! There's no way you're going to convince me that— *(Seeing something in the wing)* Oh my god! They're here!

*(*MATT *and* REED *see what* AUSTIN *sees. They all look front and scream with excitement.* MATT *and* REED *run off.)*

AUSTIN: Could I get a special light?

(A special comes up.)

AUSTIN: Ladies and gentlemen, I have some amazing news! One of the acts scheduled to perform tonight has actually arrived! *(Looks up)* Thank you, Jesus! We'll just give them a moment to set up…and while we're waiting, I'll just let you know if you want to find out more about us, you can go to the theater website *(Actually say the website address)*, you can like us on Facebook, follow us on Twitter. Anyone here on LinkedIn? Neither are we. You can also get on our email mailing list; it's a great mailing list to be on because we never send you anything. And we also wanted to let you know that our next performance is… *(Day of week and time)* …and that we'll be running through… *(Date the show closes)*—so if you enjoyed the show please tell your friends and if you didn't, tell your enemies. *(Checking)* Okay they're ready. Ladies and gentlemen, sit back and enjoy as we conclude tonight's performance with the Billy Barty Ballet

Company and their production of *Li'l Nutzy: The Elf Nutcracker!*

(Blackout. We hear Nutcracker *music. Lights up on a black-covered table that has "Li'l Nutzy" written on the front. The guys move behind it, dressed in tiny elf costumes with small bodies and shoes on their hands. Black masking now covers the scenery behind them and they wear black skirts and headgear so that their lower bodies and shoulders disappear against the black background.)*

(They perform a silly version of The Nutcracker. *Below is a description of the dance from the original production but please feel free to choreograph your own version. For a sense of what the original moves looked like go to https://www. broadwayplaypub.com/the-plays/the-ultimate-christmas-show-abridged/)*

*(*MATT *plays Clara in tiny tutu, wig and toe shoes on his hands. She stands on point and then does a series of impossible moves. She moves one foot in a half circle against the floor, then the other foot, and then both at the same time. She gracefully lifts one leg. Then the other. Then both at the same time, seemingly floating in the air. She yawns and lays down to sleep. The music suddenly changes to something dramatic and Clara wakes. Now the Mouse King enters with* REED *as the Mouse King's head and feet, and* AUSTIN *standing behind him playing the hands. The Mouse King lifts Clara and then drops her sharply to the floor. He crosses away and then jumps in the air to attack Clara, but she does the splits and impossibly slides under The Mouse King all the way to the other side of the table. In mid-air The Mouse King changes directions and flies back towards Clara who does the splits again and slides back to her original spot. The Mouse King is frustrated but before he can strike Clara, she leaps into the air punches him repeatedly in the face with her feet and then hits him in the stomach, sending him offstage.)*

*(The music changes and Clara does a celebratory dance—
leaping across the stage in the air in slow motion and
landing on point. As she lands she loses her balance and
leans off the edge of the table at almost ninety degrees. She
leaps into the air again, slowly flying to the other side of the
table and then does hand jive moves with her feet. Finally the
music changes again as The Nutcracker marches on.* AUSTIN
plays The Nutcracker Prince's head and feet, with REED
*standing behind him playing the hands. The Nutcracker
blows Clara a kiss. They run towards each other, then bump
into one another knocking each other to the ground. They get
up and dust off. Clara jumps into the Nutcracker's arms and
kisses him on the cheek. The Nutcracker flips her through the
air and she lands on her feet. Now the Nutcracker gets an
idea and starts to wave his arms like wings, lifting himself
into the air. He gestures for Clara to do the same. She tries
but cannot fly. The Nutcracker gets another idea. He flies
over to Clara and picks her up by the back of her collar and
they fly offstage, waving goodbye and Clara blowing the
audience a kiss.)*

(Blackout. Lights up. REED *runs on.)*

REED: One more hand for the Billy Barty Ballet
Company!

AUSTIN: *(Running on)* Reed! I just got great news.
Gladys said that the storm has passed, the roads
are clear, and we're all going to be able to get home
tonight! So the only thing left to say is—

*(*MATT *runs and plays a G7 chord.)*

AUSTIN: One-two-three-four!

ALL: *(Singing)*
C
Happy Merry Chrismakwanukkahanzukkah
　　　　　　　　G7
That's the only thing you'll ever have to say
　　　　C

Happy Merry Chrismakwanukkahanzukkah
   Dm7   **G7**
Wishes everyone a jolly holiday!
C
Happy Merry Chrismakwanukkahanzukkah
   F   **Bb**
If you wanna spread some universal cheer, say
G7 C   **A**
Happy Merry Chrismakwanukkahanzukkah
     Dm7
You know you wannakah...
    G7
Because it's funukkah...
  F   **Dm7** **G7**
Everyonukah...

*(They've strolled over to the Christmas tree. Reed tightens
one bulb and all the Christmas lights—on the tree, around
the stage, and all around the theatre—blaze on.)*

ALL:
    C
...This year!
Christmas come and we wan' go ho-ome!

*(Blackout. The lights come up and the guys bow as snow
falls.)*

END OF SHOW